Come get your Fudge

40 tasty and Crea

Ev

BY

MOLLY MILLS

Copyright © 2019 by Molly Mills

License Notes

No part of this book may be copied, replicated, distributed, sold or shared without the express and written consent of the Author.

The ideas expressed in the book are for entertainment purposes. The Reader assumes all risk when following any guidelines and the Author accepts no responsibility if damages occur due to actions taken by the Reader.

An Amazing Offer for Buying My Book!

Thank you very much for purchasing my books! As a token of my appreciation, I would like to extend an amazing offer to you! When you have subscribed with your e-mail address, you will have the opportunity to get free and discounted e-books that will show up in your inbox daily. You will also receive reminders before an offer expires so you never miss out. With just little effort on your part, you will have access to the newest and most informative books at your fingertips. This is all part of the VIP treatment when you subscribe below.

SIGN ME UP: *https://molly.gr8.com*

Table of Contents

Chapter I - Fruit and Nut 8

  Recipe 1: White Chocolate Coco-Macadamia Fudge 9

  Recipe 2: Maple and Walnut Fudge 11

  Recipe 3: Key Lime Fudge 14

  Recipe 4: Dark Chocolate Cranberry Cashew Fudge 16

  Recipe 5: Buttermilk Pecan Fudge 19

  Recipe 6: Strawberry Dream Fudge 22

  Recipe 7: Chocolate Almond Fudge 24

  Recipe 8: Raspberry and Coconut Fudge 27

  Recipe 9: Cranberry, Pecan, and White Chocolate Fudge 29

  Recipe 10: Nutty Vanilla Apricot Fudge 31

  Recipe 11: Fruit and Nut Milk Fudge 34

  Recipe 12: Lemon Cream Fudge 37

Recipe 13: Honey Roasted Peanut Fudge 40

Chapter II - Chocolate 42

Recipe 14: White Russian Fudge 43

Recipe 15: Mint Choc Chip Fudge 46

Recipe 16: Butterscotch Fudge 48

Recipe 17: Triple Chocolate Fudge 50

Recipe 18: Chocolate Caramel Layer Fudge 53

Recipe 19: Rocky Road Fudge 56

Recipe 20: Chocolate Fudge with Pretzels 59

Recipe 21: Pumpkin Fudge 62

Recipe 22: Cookies n Crème Fudge 65

Recipe 23: Peanut Butter and Chocolate Fudge 67

Recipe 24: Dark Chocolate Rum and Raisin 70

Recipe 25: Old-Fashioned Chocolate Fudge 72

Recipe 26: Irish Cream Fudge 74

Chapter III - Herbs and Spices 76

Recipe 27: White Cranberry Walnut Nutmeg Fudge 77

Recipe 28: Basil Fudge 80

Recipe 29: Chocolate Curry and Toasted Coconut Fudge 82

Recipe 30: Cayenne Fudge 85

Recipe 31: Caliente! A spicy hot fudge to tantalize your taste buds. 88

Recipe 32: Cinnamon Fudge Triangles 91

Recipe 33: Rosewater and Cardamom Fudge 94

Recipe 34: Coriander Fudge 97

Recipe 35: Pumpkin Fudge with Sage Caramel 99

Recipe 36: Lavender Fudge 102

Recipe 37: Persimmon Raspberry Fudge with Turmeric 105

Recipe 38: Lavender Rosemary Fudge 108

Recipe 39: Mixed Spice Raisin Fudge 111

Recipe 40: Mango and Saffron Fudge......................... 114

About the Author 116

Don't Miss Out!... 118

Chapter I - Fruit and Nut

AAAAAAAAAAAAAAAAAAAAAAAAAAAAAAAAAAAAAAAAAAAAA

Recipe 1: White Chocolate Coco-Macadamia Fudge

This sweet and nutty white fudge would make a beautiful holiday gift.

Makes: 15-20

Preparation Time: 15 minutes

Total Cooking Time: 2 hours 15 minutes

List of Ingredients:

- 1½ pounds baking white chocolate
- 1 can condensed milk sweetened
- ¼ teaspoons sea salt
- 2½ teaspoons coconut extract
- 1 cup macadamia nuts (roughly chopped)
- ½ cup coconut flakes

AAAAAAAAAAAAAAAAAAAAAAAAAAAAAAAAAAAAAAAAAAAAAA

Instructions:

1. In a double boiler, melt together the white chocolate, condensed milk, and sea salt.

2. Take off the heat and add in the coconut extract and chopped nuts.

3. Transfer the fudge into a lined rectangular loaf tin and sprinkle the flaked coconut over the top.

4. Refrigerate for at least 2 hours before slicing and serving.

Recipe 2: Maple and Walnut Fudge

Melted marshmallows bring sweetness and fluffiness to this yummy maple walnut fudge.

Makes: 18-20

Preparation Time: 15 minutes

Total Cooking Time: 2 hours 25 minutes

List of Ingredients:

- 4 cups sugar
- ½ cup salted butter
- ¾ cup pure maple syrup
- 1 cup whole milk
- 1½ cups mini marshmallows
- 1½ cups walnuts (chopped)
- 1 teaspoon vanilla

Instructions:

1. Line 2 loaf tins with parchment paper.

2. Melt together the sugar, salted butter, whole milk, and marshmallows. Heat until a candy thermometer reads 230 °F.

3. Take off the heat. When the mixture cools to 115 °F, then add in the chopped nuts and vanilla.

4. Whisk the mixture with an electric mixer until it is no longer glossy and starts to become more solid.

5. Transfer the mixture to the loaf tins. Refrigerate for at least 2 hours before slicing.

Recipe 3: Key Lime Fudge

Your favorite summer dessert in fudge form.

Makes: 16-18

Preparation Time: 15 minutes

Total Cooking Time: 6 hours 15 minutes

List of Ingredients:

- 5 ounces evaporated milk
- 1⅔ cup sugar
- ½ teaspoons salt
- 12 jumbo marshmallows (sliced in half)
- 2 cups white chocolate chips
- Zest and juice of 5 limes

Instructions:

1. Line a square baking tin with parchment paper.

2. In a saucepan, bring to boil the evaporated milk, sugar, and salt. Allow the mixture to boil for 7-8 minutes, stirring continuously. Take off the heat and add in the sliced marshmallows, chocolate chips, lime zest, and lime juice. Stir until all ingredients are combined.

3. Transfer the mix into the baking tin and refrigerate for approximately 6 hours or until set.

Recipe 4: Dark Chocolate Cranberry Cashew Fudge

Sharp cranberries combined with crunchy salted cashews make a decadent fudge that all the family can enjoy.

Makes: 36

Preparation Time: 15 minutes

Total Cooking Time: 5 hours 15 minutes

List of Ingredients:

- 12 ounces dark chocolate chips
- 1 cup sweetened condensed milk
- ⅔ cup roasted, salted cashews
- ½ cup dried cranberries
- 1 teaspoon vanilla extract

AAAAAAAAAAAAAAAAAAAAAAAAAAAAAAAAAAAAAAAAAAAAAA

Instructions:

1. Coat an 8" square baking tin with nonstick cooking spray and line with greaseproof paper. Allow a 2-3" overhang all around the tine.

2. In a medium sized saucepan over low heat, combine the chocolate chips and condensed milk. Stir continuously until the chocolate chips have completely melted. The mixture should be silky. This should take around 5-6 minutes. Add the cashews, dried cranberries, and vanilla extract. Stir to combine.

3. Pour the mixture into the prepared baking tin, spreading evenly using a spatula. Transfer the fudge to the refrigerator for 5 hours. When the fudge has set, cut the fudge into bite size squares.

Recipe 5: Buttermilk Pecan Fudge

Tangy buttermilk stops this nutty fudge from being overly sweet.

Makes: 16

Preparation Time: 30 minutes

Total Cooking Time: 1 hour 30 minutes

List of Ingredients:

- 1 cup whole pecans
- 2 cups white sugar
- 1 cup buttermilk
- ½ cup unsalted butter (chopped into pieces)
- 1 tablespoon honey
- ⅛ teaspoons sea salt (plus extra)

AAAAAAAAAAAAAAAAAAAAAAAAAAAAAAAAAAAAAAAAAAAAAAAA

Instructions:

1. Preheat your oven to 350 °F. Line a rectangular loaf tin with parchment paper, use enough that there is an excess hanging over the sides.

2. Toast the pecans in the oven for 9-10 minutes or until they become fragrant and deeper in color. When cool, roughly chop them.

3. In a saucepan, heat together the white sugar, buttermilk, unsalted butter, honey, and sea salt. Stir for 10-11 minutes until a candy thermometer reads 238 °F. Immediately transfer the mixture to a clean bowl and whisk with an electric mixer for 7-8 minutes until the mixture is cool, thick, and no longer glossy.

4. Fold in the chopped pecans, then sprinkle a little more sea salt over the top. Allow the fudge to sit for an hour at room temperature before slicing and enjoying.

Recipe 6: Strawberry Dream Fudge

It's not just its flavor that makes this strawberry fudge a dream. It is an extremely simple fudge to make.

Makes: 12-14

Preparation Time: 10 minutes

Total Cooking Time: 3 hours 10 minutes

List of Ingredients:

- 16 ounces pre-prepared strawberry frosting
- 12 ounces white chocolate chips

AAAAAAAAAAAAAAAAAAAAAAAAAAAAAAAAAAAAAAAAAAAA

Instructions:

1. Line a square baking tin with parchment paper.

2. Melt together the frosting and chocolate chips in the microwave (removing at intervals to stir).

3. When smooth, transfer the mixture to the baking tin and smooth the surface with the back of a spoon.

4. Refrigerate for a few hours or until firm enough to slice.

Recipe 7: Chocolate Almond Fudge

This is a great almond fudge for all those nut lovers out there. It's always super quick to make, too.

Makes: 36

Preparation Time: 10 minutes

Total Cooking Time: 3 hours 10 minutes

List of Ingredients:

- 2½ cups sugar
- ½ cup butter
- 1 (5-ounce) can evaporated milk
- 1 (12-ounce) package semi-sweet chocolate chips
- ¾ cup slivered almonds (roasted)
- 1 teaspoon vanilla extract

AAAAAAAAAAAAAAAAAAAAAAAAAAAAAAAAAAAAAAAAAAAAAAAA

Instructions:

1. Coat a 9" square baking tin with nonstick cooking spray and line with greaseproof paper. Allow a 2-3" overhang all round.

2. In a large saucepan, combine the sugar, butter, and milk. Bring to a quick boil on medium heat while stirring continuously. Allow the mixture to boil for 4-5 minutes while still stirring.

3. Take the pan from the heat. Add the chocolate chips and stir until the mixture is silky. Next, add the roasted almonds and vanilla extract. Stir some more.

4. Transfer the mixture to the pre-prepared baking tin and cover. Refrigerate for 2-3 hours. When the fudge is set, cut into 36 squares.

Recipe 8: Raspberry and Coconut Fudge

Raspberry and coconut are a classic flavor combination for a reason.

Makes: 16

Preparation Time: 5 minutes

Total Cooking Time: 2 hours 5 minutes

List of Ingredients:

- 1 cup coconut butter
- ¼ cup melted coconut oil
- 1½ Tablespoons pure maple syrup
- ¾ cup raspberries (pureed)

Instructions:

1. Line a square baking tin with parchment paper.

2. In a double boiler, melt the coconut butter, coconut oil, and maple syrup. Stir until totally combined and smooth. Transfer the mixture to the baking tin.

3. Drizzle the raspberry puree over the surface of the fudge then take a toothpick and swirl it through the puree and fudge to produce a marbled effect.

4. Freeze for 1-2 hours before slicing and serving.

Recipe 9: Cranberry, Pecan, and White Chocolate Fudge

Tart dried cranberries, crunchy chopped pecans, and creamy white chocolate make this fudge a winning combination.

Makes: 15-20

Preparation Time: 10 minutes

Total Cooking Time: 2 hours 25 minutes

List of Ingredients:

- 3 cups white chocolate chips
- 14 ounces sweetened condensed milk
- ¼ teaspoons salt
- 1 teaspoon vanilla extract
- ½ cup cranberries (dried)
- ½ cup pecans (roughly chopped)

AAAAAAAAAAAAAAAAAAAAAAAAAAAAAAAAAAAAAAAAAAAAAA

Instructions:

1. Line a square tin with parchment and spray with non-stick cooking spray.

2. Melt together the chocolate chips, condensed milk, and salt in a saucepan. Stir until the mixture is completely silky-smooth. Then, take it off the heat.

3. Stir in the vanilla extract, dried cranberries, and chopped pecans.

4. Refrigerate for at least 2 hours before slicing and serving.

Recipe 10: Nutty Vanilla Apricot Fudge

A cinnamon spiced milk base is perfect for candied fruit and toasted nuts.

Makes: 16-18

Preparation Time: 10 minutes

Total Cooking Time: 8 hours 10 minutes

List of Ingredients:

- 12 ounces white chocolate (roughly chopped)
- ¾ cup sweetened condensed milk
- 1 cup toasted pecans (roughly chopped)
- ½ cup dried apricots (roughly chopped)
- ½ cup dried sweet cranberries
- 2 teaspoons orange zest
- 1 teaspoon vanilla extract

Instructions:

1. Line a baking tin with parchment paper allowing a little overhang.

2. Melt together the chocolate and condensed milk in the microwave. Remove and stir until smooth and glossy.

3. Add in a ¾ cup of pecans, ¼ cup of apricots, ¼ cup of cranberries, the orange zest, and vanilla. Mix well so that all ingredients are evenly distributed.

4. Transfer the mixture to the baking tin and scatter the remaining fruit and nuts over the top. Refrigerate overnight before slicing.

Recipe 11: Fruit and Nut Milk Fudge

A cinnamon-spiced milk base is perfect for candied fruit and toasted nuts.

Makes: 18-20

Preparation Time: 20 minutes

Total Cooking Time: 8 hours 20 minutes

List of Ingredients:

- 4 cups white sugar
- 2 cups whole milk
- 1 cinnamon stick
- ½ cup light corn syrup
- ¼ teaspoons baking soda
- ¼ teaspoons kosher salt
- 8 Tablespoons butter, unsalted
- 2 teaspoons vanilla
- 1 cup assorted candied fruit (chopped into small pieces)
- ½ cup toasted pecans (chopped)
- ½ cup toasted walnuts (chopped)
- ½ cup toasted pine nuts (chopped)

Instructions:

1. In a medium saucepan, simmer the sugar, whole milk, cinnamon stick, corn syrup, baking soda, and kosher salt. Mix well and allow it to get to a temperature of 235-240 °F, skimming off any foam that forms on the surface.

2. Take off the heat and add in the butter and vanilla. Don't stir the mixture yet. Remove the cinnamon stick. Allow the mixture to cool to 175-180 °F.

3. In the meantime, line a square baking tin with parchment paper.

4. Stir the cooled mixture until it loses its gloss and starts to become more solid. Transfer the fudge to the baking tin and refrigerate overnight before slicing into cubes.

Recipe 12: Lemon Cream Fudge

Since this fudge is bursting with a zesty lemon flavor, it is the perfect sweet treat for summer.

Makes: 16

Preparation Time: 10 minutes

Total Cooking Time: 3 hours 10 minutes

List of Ingredients:

- 2¼ cups white sugar
- ¾ cup evaporated milk
- 8 ounces white chocolate chips
- ½ cup salted butter
- 4 teaspoons extract of lemon
- Zest of 1 fresh lemon
- Yellow food dye

Instructions:

1. Line a square baking tin with parchment paper.

2. Bring the sugar and evaporated milk to a boil, then reduce the heat a little. Stir until a candy thermometer reads 230-235 °F.

3. Take off the heat and immediately stir in the white chocolate chips, salted butter, lemon extract, and lemon zest. When melted and smooth, add a few drops of yellow food dye. Mix a final time, then transfer the fudge to the baking tin.

4. Allow the mixture to stand at room temperature for 2-3 hours before serving.

Recipe 13: Honey Roasted Peanut Fudge

This addictive sweet fudge is studded with honey roasted peanuts for extra crunch.

Makes: 24

Preparation Time: 10 minutes

Total Cooking Time: 2 hours 10 minutes

List of Ingredients:

- ⅔ cup evaporated milk
- 1½ cups white sugar
- 2 Tablespoons salted butter
- 2 cups of mini marshmallows
- 2 cups white chocolate chips
- 1½ cups honey roasted peanuts
- 2 teaspoons vanilla extract

Instructions:

1. Line a square baking tin with parchment paper.

2. In a heavy saucepan, bring to boil the white sugar, evaporated milk, and salted butter. Allow the mixture to boil for 4-5 minutes before taking off the heat.

3. Add in the marshmallows, chocolate chips, 1 cup of peanuts, and vanilla. Stir well until the marshmallows and chocolate chips have melted. Transfer the mix to the baking tin. Sprinkle the remaining peanuts over top of the fudge and refrigerate for at least 2 hours before serving.

Chapter II - Chocolate

AAAAAAAAAAAAAAAAAAAAAAAAAAAAAAAAAAAAAAAAAAAAAA

Recipe 14: White Russian Fudge

All your favorite White Russian ingredients are here in this fudge. With vanilla vodka and coffee liqueur, this fudge packs a serious punch.

Makes: 16-18

Preparation Time: 15 minutes

Total Cooking Time: 2 hours 15 minutes

List of Ingredients:

- 2 cups white sugar
- 4 ounces unsalted butter
- ⅓ cup heavy cream
- 2 Tablespoons vanilla vodka
- ¼ cup & 2tbsp coffee liqueur
- 2 cups white chocolate chips
- 7 ounces marshmallow fluff
- 1 teaspoon vanilla
- Chocolate sprinkles (for decoration)

Instructions:

1. Line a square baking tin with parchment paper.

2. In a heavy saucepan, combine the white sugar, unsalted butter, cream, vodka, and liqueur. Bring to a boil and leave (stirring continuously) for 8-10 minutes or until a candy thermometer reads 233-235 °F.

3. Take off the heat and immediately stir in the chocolate chips until the mixture is smooth. Then, add in the marshmallow fluff and vanilla. Mix well until all the ingredients are combined.

4. Transfer to the baking tin and top with chocolate sprinkles. Allow the fudge to sit at room temperature for 2 hours before slicing and serving.

Recipe 15: Mint Choc Chip Fudge

This refreshing minty fudge is a great treat to serve with after dinner coffee.

Makes: 16

Preparation Time: 5 minutes

Total Cooking Time: 2 hours 5 minutes

List of Ingredients:

- 3¼ cups white chocolate chips
- 2 Tablespoons salted butter
- 1 can sweetened condensed milk
- 2½ teaspoons mint extract
- Green food dye
- ¾ cup mini milk chocolate chips

Instructions:

1. Line a square baking tin with parchment paper.

2. Melt the white chocolate chips and butter together in the microwave. Stir until smooth and glossy.

3. Add in the condensed milk and mint extract. Mix well then add a few drops of green food dye. Allow the mixture to cool for 5 minutes before folding through the mini milk chocolate chips.

4. Transfer the fudge to the baking tin. Refrigerate the fudge for at least 2 hours before slicing into bite-sized pieces.

Recipe 16: Butterscotch Fudge

With as few as 5 ingredients and only 9 minutes of preparation, this candy treat is good to go!

Makes: 24

Preparation Time: 9 minutes

Total Cooking Time: 2 hours 9 minutes

List of Ingredients:

- 1 (14 ounce) can sweetened condensed milk
- 1 (11 ounce) package butterscotch chips
- 6 ounces white chocolate chips
- 1 teaspoon butter flavor extract
- 1 teaspoon rum flavor extract

Instructions:

1. In a medium saucepan, combine the first 3 ingredients. Melt them over medium heat until the mixture is smooth. Stir well. Remove the mixture from the heat, then add the butter flavoring and the rum flavoring one at a time.

2. Transfer the mixture into a 9x13" baking dish lined with grease-proof paper. Refrigerate for 1-2 hours or until set.

3. When solid, remove the baking dish from the refrigerator. Cut the fudge into 24 bite sized pieces.

Recipe 17: Triple Chocolate Fudge

Wow, there are three different types of chocolate in every delicious bite. This fudge is a chocoholics dream.

Makes: 75

Preparation Time: 30 minutes

Total Cooking Time: 3 hours 30 minutes

List of Ingredients:

- 3⅓ cups white sugar
- 1 cup packed dark brown sugar
- 1 can (12 ounces) evaporated milk
- 1 cup butter (cubed)
- 32 large marshmallows (halved)
- 1 teaspoon vanilla extract
- 2 cups (12 ounces) semisweet chocolate chips
- 14 ounces milk chocolate (chopped)
- 2 ounces semisweet chocolate (chopped)
- 2 cups chopped pecans (toasted)

AAAAAAAAAAAAAAAAAAAAAAAAAAAAAAAAAAAAAAAAAAAAA

Instructions:

1. Coat a 15x10x1" baking tin with nonstick cooking spray and line with greaseproof paper. Allow a 2-3" overhang all round.

2. In a heavy saucepan, combine the white sugar, brown sugar, evaporated milk, and butter. Bring the pan to a boil over medium heat. Stir continuously and boil for around 4-5 minutes. Remove the pan from the heat. Add the marshmallows and vanilla extract. Stir the mixture well to blend.

3. A little at a time stir in the chocolate chips, the milk chocolate, and the semisweet chocolate. Stir well until everything is totally melted. Next, fold in the toasted pecans. Spread the mixture into the prepared tin smoothing the top with a spatula to even it out.

4. Transfer the tin to a refrigerator for 2-3 hours or until set. Cut the fudge into 1" squares when solid.

Recipe 18: Chocolate Caramel Layer Fudge

As good to look at as it is to eat. This is a great treat to serve at a dinner party.

Makes: 18

Preparation Time: 15 minutes

Total Cooking Time: 8 hours 15 minutes

List of Ingredients:

- 4 Tablespoons salted butter
- 3 cups good quality milk chocolate chips
- 1 can sweetened, full-fat, condensed milk
- 2 teaspoons vanilla extract
- 25 caramel candies
- 2 Tablespoons heavy cream
- ¼ teaspoons sea salt

AAAAAAAAAAAAAAAAAAAAAAAAAAAAAAAAAAAAAAAAAAAAAAAA

Instructions:

1. Line a square baking tin with parchment paper.

2. Melt the butter and chocolate chips together in the microwave. Add the condensed milk and vanilla, then microwave for a further 40 seconds, pausing halfway to stir. If the mixture has not completely melted, then microwave it for a little extra time. Transfer the mix into the baking tin.

3. In a clean bowl, add the caramel candies and heavy cream. Melt this mixture in the microwave. Stir until smooth, then pour over the chocolate layer in the baking tin. Sprinkle a little sea salt over the surface and refrigerate overnight before serving.

Recipe 19: Rocky Road Fudge

Turkish Delight and mini mallows make for a delicious fudge version of Rocky Road.

Makes: 16

Preparation Time: 5 minutes

Total Cooking Time: 4 hours 5 minutes

List of Ingredients:

- 10½ ounces milk chocolate melts
- 1 (14 ounces) can have condensed milk
- 1-ounce unsalted butter (chopped)
- 1½ cups mini marshmallows
- ½ cup roasted and salted peanuts
- 4 ounces Turkish Delight bars (any brand)

Instructions:

1. Coat an 8" square baking tin with nonstick cooking spray and line with greaseproof paper. Allow a 2-3" overhang all round.

2. In a microwave-safe bowl, combine the chocolate melts, condensed milk, and butter. Microwave on half power in bursts of 30 seconds, stir the chocolate with a dry spoon after each burst. When the chocolates have melted together (which should take around 2-3 minutes) stir in the marshmallows, salted peanuts, and chunks of Turkish Delight.

3. Pour the fudge into the prepared tin and smooth over the top with a spatula.

4. Transfer the fudge to the refrigerator for 3-4 hours or until completely solid. When set, cut into bite size pieces.

Recipe 20: Chocolate Fudge with Pretzels

Salty pretzels give a great contrast of flavor and crunch to this sweet chocolatey fudge.

Makes: 18-20

Preparation Time: 15 minutes

Total Cooking Time: 3 hours 15 minutes

List of Ingredients:

- Non-stick cooking spray
- 2 Tablespoons unsalted butter (cut into small pieces)
- 3 cups semisweet chocolate chips
- 1 can (14 ounces) sweetened condensed milk
- ½ teaspoons pure vanilla extract
- ⅛ teaspoons fine salt
- 2½ cups miniature pretzels (roughly chopped)

AAAAAAAAAAAAAAAAAAAAAAAAAAAAAAAAAAAAAAAAAAAAAA

Instructions:

1. Coat an 8" square baking tin with non-stick cooking spray, then line with greaseproof paper. Allow a 2-3" overhang.

2. Combine the butter, chocolate chips, milk, vanilla extract, and salt in a heatproof bowl. Put the bowl over a pot of lightly simmering water. Stir a few times to ensure that the chocolate melts and that the mixture is combined. The mixture should be warm rather than hot. This should take around 7-10 minutes.

3. Remove the bowl from the heat and add 2 cups of pretzels. Spoon the mixture into the baking tin. Smooth the top using a knife. Press the remaining ½ cup of pretzels on top. Transfer the baking tin to the refrigerator and allow the mixture to set for 2-3 hours.

4. When the fudge is the desired consistency, remove it carefully from the pan by lifting it out using the greaseproof paper. Cut into 36 uniform squares.

Recipe 21: Pumpkin Fudge

Why not make this fudge for Thanksgiving?

Makes: 18-20

Preparation Time: 20 minutes

Total Cooking Time: 8 hours 30 minutes

List of Ingredients:

- 3 cups white sugar
- 1 cup whole milk
- 3 Tablespoons light corn syrup
- ½ cup pumpkin puree
- ¼ teaspoons sea salt
- 1 teaspoon pumpkin pie spice
- 1½ teaspoons vanilla extract
- ½ cup butter
- ½ cup walnuts (chopped)

AAAAAAAAAAAAAAAAAAAAAAAAAAAAAAAAAAAAAAAAAAAAAAA

Instructions:

1. Coat an 8" square baking tin with non-stick cooking spray, then line it with greaseproof paper. Allow a 2-3" overhang all round.

2. In a large saucepan, combine the sugar, whole milk, light corn syrup, pumpkin puree, and sea salt. Bring the pan to a boil while continuously stirring. When it begins boiling, immediately reduce the heat to medium. Allow the mixture to gently boil but stop stirring it.

3. Take a candy thermometer and when the mixture reaches 230 °F, remove the pan from the heat. If you don't have a thermometer, then drop some of the mixture into cold water. If it forms a ball, then it is ready. Remove the pan from the heat. Stir in the pumpkin spice, vanilla extract, butter, and walnuts. Set the pan aside to cool.

4. Vigorously beat the mixture until it is thick and has lost a little bit of its shine. Transfer it to the pre-prepared baking tin.

5. When set, cut the fudge into 36 bite size squares.

Recipe 22: Cookies n Crème Fudge

Everyone loves cookies, so this fudge is sure to be a winner.

Makes: 40

Preparation Time: 10 minutes

Total Cooking Time: 3 hours 10 minutes

List of Ingredients:

- 18 ounces white chocolate baking squares
- 1 (14 ounce) can sweetened condensed milk
- ⅛ teaspoons sea salt
- 3 cups cookies n crème biscuits (coarsely crushed)

AAAAAAAAAAAAAAAAAAAAAAAAAAAAAAAAAAAAAAAAAAAA

Instructions:

1. In a large saucepan, combine the chocolate squares, condensed milk, and sea salt. Melt over a low heat. When totally melted remove the pan from the heat and add the crushed biscuits. Stir well to combine.

2. Transfer the mixture to an 8" square baking tin, lined with greaseproof paper. Chill the tin in the refrigerator for 2-3 hours, until solid.

3. When completely set pop the fudge out of the pan onto a clean work surface or board. Cut into 40 bite size squares.

Recipe 23: Peanut Butter and Chocolate Fudge

Peanut butter and chocolate are always a match made in heaven.

Makes: 20

Preparation Time: 15 minutes

Total Cooking Time: 2 hours 15 minutes

List of Ingredients:

- 1 cup coconut butter
- ½ cup pure maple syrup
- 1½ cups smooth peanut butter
- 1 teaspoon vanilla extract
- 14 ounces dark baking chocolate

Instructions:

1. Line a square baking tin with parchment paper.

2. Melt together the coconut butter, maple syrup, peanut butter, and vanilla in a microwave. Stir well until the mixture is smooth and pourable. Set aside.

3. In a separate bowl, melt the dark chocolate in the microwave. Stir well and set aside.

4. Transfer half of the melted peanut butter mixture into the lined baking tin. Smooth the surface with the back of a spoon.

5. Add the melted milk chocolate to the remaining half of the peanut butter mixture, and stir well. Pour on top of the bottom layer in the tin. Smooth the surface with the back of a clean spoon. Refrigerate the fudge for at least 2 hours before slicing into pieces.

Recipe 24: Dark Chocolate Rum and Raisin

The UK's most popular fudge flavor. It's a classic for a reason!

Makes: 16-18

Preparation Time: 10 minutes

Total Cooking Time: 3 hours 10 minutes

List of Ingredients:

- 14 ounces dark chocolate
- 1 can condensed milk
- ½ cup raisins
- 1 teaspoon rum flavoring

AAAAAAAAAAAAAAAAAAAAAAAAAAAAAAAAAAAAAAAAAAAAAA

Instructions:

1. Line a square baking tin with parchment paper.

2. Melt together the dark chocolate and condensed milk in a microwave.

3. Remove the mixture from the microwave and mix well. Then, add in the raisins and rum flavoring. Give a final good stir before transferring the mixture to the baking tin and refrigerating for 2-3 hours. Slice and serve when set.

Recipe 25: Old-Fashioned Chocolate Fudge

This classic chocolate fudge recipe may be simple but it certainly isn't boring.

Makes: 20-25

Preparation Time: 15 minutes

Total Cooking Time: 2 hours 10 minutes

List of Ingredients:

- 2 cups sugar
- ½ cup cocoa
- 1 cup whole milk
- 4 Tablespoons salted butter
- 1 teaspoon vanilla

AAAAAAAAAAAAAAAAAAAAAAAAAAAAAAAAAAAAAAAAAAAAA

Instructions:

1. Line a square baking tin with parchment paper.

2. In a heavy saucepan, bring to a boil the sugar, cocoa and whole milk. Stir continuously until a candy thermometer reads 234 °F. Take the pan off the heat, then add in the salted butter and vanilla. Stir until the mixture becomes matte and starts to become more solid.

3. Transfer the fudge into the baking tin and allow it to reach room temperature before slicing and serving.

Recipe 26: Irish Cream Fudge

Irish cream liqueur blended with milk chocolate can make a dreamy and totally addictive fudge.

Makes: 16-18

Preparation Time: 5 minutes

Total Cooking Time: 4 hours 5 minutes

List of Ingredients:

- 21 ounces milk choc chips
- 1 cup condensed milk, sweetened
- ¼ cup Irish cream liqueur
- 1 teaspoon vanilla

AAAAAAAAAAAAAAAAAAAAAAAAAAAAAAAAAAAAAAAAAAAAAA

Instructions:

1. Line a square baking tin with parchment paper.

2. Melt together the milk choc chips and condensed milk in the microwave.

3. Take out of the microwave, stir well and then pour in the Irish cream liqueur and vanilla. Give a final mix until totally smooth before transferring into the baking tin and refrigerating for 4 hours. Slice and serve when set.

Chapter III - Herbs and Spices

AAAAAAAAAAAAAAAAAAAAAAAAAAAAAAAAAAAAAAAAA

Recipe 27: White Cranberry Walnut Nutmeg Fudge

Creamy white chocolate, sharp cranberries and crunchy walnut all combine to make a decadent treat.

Makes: 24

Preparation Time: 4 minutes

Total Cooking Time: 8 hours 4 minutes

List of Ingredients:

- 1 teaspoon butter
- 3 cups white chocolate chips
- 1 (14 ounce) can sweetened condensed milk
- ⅓ cup butter
- 2 teaspoons rum flavoring
- 1 teaspoon vanilla extract
- ¼ teaspoons ground nutmeg
- 1 cup sweetened dried cranberries
- 1 cup walnuts (broken)

Instructions:

1. Lightly grease a 9" square baking tin with the teaspoon of butter.

2. Combine the chocolate chips, milk, and butter in a microwaveable bowl. Microwave in 25-second intervals on high heat. Stir between intervals. It is done when the chocolate is completely melted. This will take around 3 minutes.

3. Next, add the rum flavoring, vanilla, and nutmeg. Fold in the dried cranberries and broken pieces of walnut. Pour the fudge into the pre-prepared baking tin.

4. Allow the fudge to cool and set overnight before cutting into squares.

Recipe 28: Basil Fudge

Basil is becoming more popular as an ingredient in candy and cakes. In fact, it's safe to say it is the new lavender!

Makes: 12

Preparation Time: 10 minutes

Total Cooking Time: 3 hours 20 minutes

List of Ingredients:

- 2½ ounces butter
- 1 tin sweetened condensed milk
- 15 ounces dark chocolate melts
- 1 handful of fresh basil leaves (chopped)

AAAAAAAAAAAAAAAAAAAAAAAAAAAAAAAAAAAAAAAAAAAAAA

Instructions:

1. Coat an 8" square baking tin with nonstick cooking spray and line with greaseproof paper. Allow a 2-3" overhang all round

2. Melt the butter in a medium saucepan on the medium-low heat and add the condensed milk and chocolate. Stir continuously until the chocolate has totally melted. Turn the heat off and add the chopped basil leaves.

3. Pour the fudge into the prepared baking tin and place it in the refrigerator for 2-3 hours or until the fudge has set.

4. When set, cut into bite size squares.

Recipe 29: Chocolate Curry and Toasted Coconut Fudge

Sugar, spice, and everything nice!

Makes: 10

Preparation Time: 10 minutes

Total Cooking Time: 2 hours 10 minutes

List of Ingredients:

- ½ cup sweetened shredded coconut
- ½ cup salted butter
- ½ cup whole fat coconut cream
- 1 cup cacao powder
- ½ cup heavy cream
- ½ cup white sugar
- 1 teaspoon curry powder
- 2 Tablespoons shredded coconut
- Sea salt

AAAAAAAAAAAAAAAAAAAAAAAAAAAAAAAAAAAAAAAAAAAAA

Instructions:

1. In a large non-stick pan over a medium heat, toast the shredded coconut. Toss the coconut every 25 seconds or so until it is golden. This should take around 4 minutes. Set the pan aside.

2. Heat a medium sized saucepan filled with 1-2" of water over high heat. Bring the water to the boil. In a medium metal mixing bowl a little larger than the saucepan, combine the butter and coconut cream. Place the mixing bowl on top of the pan containing the boiling water. Do not allow the mixing bowl to come into direct contact with the water. When the butter and coconut have melted, remove from the bowl from the heat. Set aside to cool for no more than 40 seconds.

3. Next, stir in the cacao powder. Should the ingredients start to show signs of separating wait a few seconds more to allow it to cool a little bit more. When you are confident the mixture is cool enough, stir in the heavy cream, curry powder, and shredded coconut. Stir until totally blended.

4. Pour the mixture into a greaseproof paper lined loaf tin. Sprinkle with sea salt and place in the refrigerator for 1-2 hours.

5. When set, remove from refrigerator and cut into square bite size pieces. Sprinkle the finished squares with shredded coconut.

Recipe 30: Cayenne Fudge

This little piece of candy certainly packs a punch!

Makes: 12

Preparation Time: 10 minutes

Total Cooking Time: 55 minutes

List of Ingredients:

- ½ cup almond milk
- 2 Tablespoons margarine
- 4 cups confectioners' sugar
- 1 cup dark chocolate chips
- ½ cup cocoa powder
- ½ teaspoons vanilla extract
- ½ teaspoons ground cinnamon
- ½ teaspoons cayenne pepper

Instructions:

1. Lightly grease an 8" square glass baking dish.

2. In a medium saucepan, combine the milk and margarine over a medium heat. Bring to a simmer for around 4-5 minutes. In a medium sized mixing bowl, combine the sugar, chocolate chips, cocoa powder, vanilla, ground cinnamon, and cayenne pepper. Pour this mixture into the prepared glass baking dish. Then add the hot milk mixture over the sugar mixture and spread evenly.

3. Place the dish in the refrigerator until set. This will take around 30-40 minutes.

4. When set, cut into squares.

Recipe 31: Caliente! A spicy hot fudge to tantalize your taste buds.

Makes: 16

Preparation Time: 10 minutes

Total Cooking Time: 8 hours 10 minutes

List of Ingredients:

- 1 pound semi-sweet chocolate (chopped)
- 3 Tablespoons butter
- 1 can (14-ounces) fat-Free Sweetened Condensed Milk
- 3 Tablespoons brewed espresso
- 2 teaspoons ground cinnamon
- ⅛ teaspoons chili powder
- ⅛ teaspoons ground cayenne pepper
- Sea salt

Instructions:

1. Coat an 8" square baking tin with nonstick cooking spray and line with greaseproof paper. Allow a 2-3" overhang all round. Set aside.

2. Fill a medium sized saucepan with cold water. It will need to be around 2" deep. Bring the water to a simmer.

3. In a medium mixing bowl (one a little bigger than the saucepan), combine the chocolate, butter, milk, and espresso. Place the bowl on top of the pan containing the simmering water. Make sure that the mixing bowl doesn't come into contact with the water. Stir continuously until the chocolate is totally melted and silky. Add the 3 spices, then remove from the heat and pour the mixture into the baking tin.

4. Scatter sea salt on top of the fudge and chill in the refrigerator overnight.

5. Cut into squares when set.

Recipe 32: Cinnamon Fudge Triangles

Spicy cinnamon is the perfect companion for a sweet, buttery fudge.

Makes: 18-20

Preparation Time: 10 minutes

Total Cooking Time: 2 hours 10 minutes

List of Ingredients:

- 3 cups confectioner's sugar
- ½ cup unsweetened cocoa powder
- ½ teaspoons ground cinnamon
- ½ cup butter
- ¼ cup milk
- 1 ½ teaspoons vanilla extract
- 1 cup walnuts (chopped)

Instructions:

1. Line an 8" square baking tin with lightly greased aluminum foil. Allow the foil to hang 2-3" over the edges.

2. In a large bowl over medium heat, combine the sugar, cocoa, and ground cinnamon. Using a medium saucepan, heat the butter and milk. As soon as the butter has melted, add the vanilla extract. Remove the pan from the heat and gradually stir in the sugar mixture. Next, add the walnuts. Pour the mixture into the prepared tin. Place in the refrigerator until firm. This should take around 1-2 hours.

3. Ease the fudge out of the tin using the aluminum foil overhang. Slice the fudge into 2" uniform square. Slice diagonally to make triangular shapes.

Recipe 33: Rosewater and Cardamom Fudge

Cardamom's citrus flavor pairs perfectly with pistachios and rosewater.

Makes: 20-24

Preparation Time: 15 minutes

Total Cooking Time: 2 hours 15 minutes

List of Ingredients:

- ½ cup & 1 tablespoon warm water
- 1¼ cups sugar
- ¼ teaspoons salt
- 1¼ cups powdered milk
- 1 teaspoon rosewater
- 1 teaspoon cardamom
- 2 Tablespoons walnuts (finely chopped)
- 2 Tablespoons almonds (finely chopped)
- 2 Tablespoons pistachios (finely chopped)

AAAAAAAAAAAAAAAAAAAAAAAAAAAAAAAAAAAAAAAAAAAAAAAA

Instructions:

1. First, lay all of the ingredients needed for this recipe on a clean work surface. Timing is crucial for this recipe, so you will need to have them all measured and at hand before starting.

2. Grease a baking pan measuring approximately 7x11" and no more than 2 inches in depth. In a heavy saucepan, add the water, sugar, and salt. Stir until the sugar totally melts or for around 4 minutes. Increase the heat to high and bring the mixture to boil, stirring constantly for around 2 minutes. Foam will form on the syrup and it will quickly thicken.

3. Remove the pan from the heat. Add the powdered milk and stir. Next, add the rosewater, cardamom, walnuts, and almonds. Stir well and make sure that the nuts are evenly distributed throughout the batter.

4. Pour the mixture into the greased baking pan and use a spatula to even it out. Scatter pistachios over the fudge and set it aside to cool. This should take around 2 hours.

5. When the fudge has set, use a sharp knife and cut it into 2" squares. Store in an airtight container. Do not store in a refrigerator.

Spicy Mexican Hot Chocolate Fudge

Recipe 34: Coriander Fudge

This is a super healthy and organic fudge that you can make in just 5 minutes. That is amazing!

Makes: 16

Preparation Time: 5 minutes

Total Cooking Time: 5 hours 5 minutes

List of Ingredients:

- ⅔ cup organic coconut oil
- ⅔ cup organic liquid honey
- ⅔ cup raw cocoa powder
- 1 teaspoon organic vanilla extract
- 1 teaspoon organic ground coriander

AAAAAAAAAAAAAAAAAAAAAAAAAAAAAAAAAAAAAAAAAAAAAA

Instructions:

1. Melt the coconut oil in a microwaveable safe bowl. Place the bowl in the microwave on high for no more than 40 seconds. Add the organic honey and raw cocoa powder and stir to combine. Next, add the vanilla extract and ground coriander. Stir well to combine.

2. Transfer the mixture to a greaseproof paper lined 8" square baking tin. Cover and place in the refrigerator for 4-5 hours.

3. When set, cut into bite size pieces.

Recipe 35: Pumpkin Fudge with Sage Caramel

A vegan fudge can be ideal as an after dinner party dessert.

Makes: 12

Preparation Time: 20 minutes

Total Cooking Time: 1hour 20 minutes

List of Ingredients:

- 1 cup almond butter
- 8 Medjool dates
- 2 Tablespoons coconut oil
- 1 tablespoon cinnamon
- ½ teaspoons ginger
- ½ teaspoons nutmeg
- ¼ teaspoons ground clove
- 1 cup organic pumpkin puree
- For the Caramel:
- 6 Medjool dates
- ¼ cup water
- Sprouted pumpkin seeds
- Sea salt

Instructions:

1. In a blender or food processor, combine the almond butter and dates. Blitz until totally blended. Add the coconut, cinnamon, ginger, nutmeg, and clove. Stir thoroughly. Next, add the pumpkin puree and blitz until silky.

2. Pour the mixture into a 6" square baking dish smoothing out the top with a spatula until even. Transfer to the refrigerator to cool.

3. For the caramel: In a small saucepan over medium heat, use ¼ cup of water and heat the Medjool dates. Stir constantly until they begin to break down to form a paste. Add more water as needed. The paste needs to be smooth and a little thick. Next, add the pumpkins seeds.

4. Spread the caramel evenly on top of the fudge and transfer to the freezer for 20-30 minutes or until set.

5. When solid, scatter chopped sage on top of the fudge and sprinkle with sea salt. Cut into bite size pieces.

Recipe 36: Lavender Fudge

Dried lavender is often used in cooking. Its unique flavor is ideal for sweets and desserts.

Makes: 20-24

Preparation Time: 40 minutes

Total Cooking Time: 5 hours 40 minutes

List of Ingredients:

- ¾ cup heavy cream
- 1 tablespoon dried lavender
- ½ cup salted butter
- 2 cups white sugar
- ¾ teaspoons salt
- 12 ounces white chocolate chips
- 7 ounces marshmallow fluff
- 1 teaspoon vanilla extract
- 3-4 drops purple food gel

AAAAAAAAAAAAAAAAAAAAAAAAAAAAAAAAAAAAAAAAAAAAAAAA

Instructions:

1. Line a 9" square pan with aluminum foil that has been sprayed with cooking spray.

2. In a small saucepan over medium heat, combine the cream and lavender. Bring the mixture to a simmer. Remove the pan from the heat, then cover it with a lid. Allow the mixture to stand and infuse for half an hour.

3. Next, pour the cream through a sieve into a large saucepan in order to remove the lavender. Add the butter, sugar, and salt to the mixture. Place the saucepan over medium heat. Stir the mixture constantly until the sugar and butter are totally melted.

4. Bring the fudge to the boil while stirring constantly. Using a candy thermometer, keep checking until the fudge reaches 235 °F. When the temperature has been reached, take the saucepan off the heat and stir in the chocolate chips and marshmallow cream until they are totally melted. You may return the fudge to the heat if necessary.

5. Add the vanilla along with 3 drops of food coloring. Stir and add a little more color until you are happy with the shade of purple. Pour the fudge into the pre-prepared pan and using the back of a spoon smooth is out. Allow the fudge to set at a room temperature for approximately 4-5 hours. Alternatively, place in the refrigerator for 1-2 hours. As soon as the fudge has set, cut it into 1" square pieces.

Recipe 37: Persimmon Raspberry Fudge with Turmeric

Despite this fudge being packed full of healthy ingredients, it will totally satisfy your sweet cravings.

Makes: 36

Preparation Time: 15 minutes

Total Cooking Time: 8 hours 15 minutes

List of Ingredients:

- 2 cups sunflower seeds
- 2 cups Medjool dates
- 3 persimmons
- 1 cup fresh raspberries
- 2-inch piece turmeric root
- 1 teaspoon ground cinnamon
- ½ teaspoons ground nutmeg
- ⅓ cup frozen raspberries
- 1 tablespoon organic cacao nibs

AAAAAAAAAAAAAAAAAAAAAAAAAAAAAAAAAAAAAAAAAA

Instructions:

1. Coat a 9" square baking tin with nonstick cooking spray and line with greaseproof paper. Allow a 2-3" overhang all round. Set aside.

2. Using a blender or food processor, blitz the sunflower seeds in order to make flour. Add the remaining 8 ingredients to the jug and blend until silky. Pour the mixture into the tin.

3. Transfer the baking tin to the refrigerator. Allow the fudge to set overnight.

4. When totally set, cut into bite-sized pieces, top with frozen raspberries, and sprinkle with cacao nibs.

Recipe 38: Lavender Rosemary Fudge

Rosemary adds a pine-like flavor to the fudge and perfectly complements the lavender.

Makes: 24

Preparation Time: 10 minutes

Total Cooking Time: 2 hours 10 minutes

List of Ingredients:

- ⅔ cup organic evaporated milk
- ½ Tablespoons dried lavender buds
- 1¼ cup cane sugar
- 5 Tablespoons butter
- 12 ounces semisweet chocolate chips
- 1½ cups mini marshmallows
- Lavender Rosemary Sea Salt

Instructions:

1. Line an 8" square baking pan with aluminum foil and put to one side.

2. In a medium sized pan over medium-high heat, add the evaporated milk, lavender buds, sugar, and butter. Whisk well to combine before bringing the mixture to a boil while constantly stirring. Boil and continuously whisk for 4-5 minutes.

3. Using a sieve, strain the mixture into a second pot. Discarding the lavender buds. Place the second pot on the heat for 30 seconds. Add the marshmallows and chocolate. Stir until both have melted and combined.

4. Pour the lavender fudge into the prepared 8" baking pan and scatter with lavender rosemary salt. Allow it to cool before cutting into squares.

Recipe 39: Mixed Spice Raisin Fudge

Raisins and mixed spice fuse together to make the perfect fudge.

Makes: 12

Preparation Time: 30 minutes

Total Cooking Time: 8 hours 30 minutes

List of Ingredients:

- 4 ounces butter
- ½ pint milk
- 2 pounds sugar
- 7-ounce tin sweetened condensed milk
- 1 teaspoon Mixed Spice
- 6 ounces raisins

Instructions:

1. Combine the butter and milk in a large saucepan that can hold 7 or 8 pints. Gently heat until all of the butter has completely melted. Stir in the sugar. When the sugar has dissolved, add the condensed milk and bring it to a boil. Allow the mixture to boil rapidly while stirring for approximately 20-25 minutes or until the mixture becomes a rich caramel color and thickens.

2. Remove the pan from the heat, then add the Mixed Spice and raisins. Vigorously beat the mixture for 4-5 minutes or until thick. Transfer the mixture into a lightly greased baking tin (7x11") and place the pan in a refrigerator. Just before the fudge is totally cold score the top with 1" squares that will allow you to easily cut it later.

3. Refrigerate overnight.

Recipe 40: Mango and Saffron Fudge

Made in the microwave with a total prep time of only 8 minutes!

Makes: 18

Preparation Time: 8 minutes

Total Cooking Time: 3 hours 8 minutes

List of Ingredients:

- 4 cups milk powder
- 1½ cups sugar
- 1 cup mango pulp
- 1¼ cups double cream
- 1 tablespoon milk masala
- A few strands of saffron

Instructions:

1. In a large microwaveable bowl, combine all the ingredients except the mango pulp. Stir and cover. Place the bowl in the microwave on high for no more than 4 minutes.

2. Remove the bowl from the microwave, then mix and transfer to a lightly greased 8" square baking tin. Cover with cling film wrap and transfer it to the refrigerator for 2-3 hours.

3. When set, cut into bite size squares.

About the Author

Molly Mills always knew she wanted to feed people delicious food for a living. Being the oldest child with three younger brothers, Molly learned to prepare meals at an early age to help out her busy parents. She just seemed to know what spice went with which meat and how to make sauces that would dress up the blandest of pastas. Her creativity in the kitchen was a blessing to a family where money was tight and making new meals every day was a challenge.

Molly was also a gifted athlete as well as chef and secured a Lacrosse scholarship to Syracuse University. This was a blessing to her family as she was the first to go to college and at little cost to her parents. She took full advantage of her college education and earned a business degree. When she graduated, she joined her culinary skills and business acumen into a successful catering business. She wrote her first e-book after a customer asked if she could pay for several of her recipes. This sparked the entrepreneurial spirit in Mills and she thought if one person wanted them, then why not share the recipes with the world!

Molly lives near her family's home with her husband and three children and still cooks for her family every chance she gets. She plays Lacrosse with a local team made up of her old teammates from college and there are always some tasty nibbles on the ready after each game.

Don't Miss Out!

Scan the QR-Code below and you can sign up to receive emails whenever Molly Mills publishes a new book. There's no charge and no obligation.

Sign Me Up

https://molly.gr8.com

Printed in Poland
by Amazon Fulfillment
Poland Sp. z o.o., Wrocław